W9-ACF-889

QUESTIONS FOR ECCLESIASTES

Published by Story Line Press, Inc., Three Oaks Farm, Brownsville, OR 97327

This publication was made possible thanks in part to the generous support of the Nicholas Roerich Museum, the Andrew W. Mellon Foundation, the National Endowment for the Arts, US West Foundation and individual contributors.

Library of Congress Cataloging-in-Publication Data
Jarman, Mark.
        Questions for Ecclesiastes : poems / by Mark Jarman. — 1st ed.
            p.   cm.
        ISBN 1-885266-42-1 (cloth). — ISBN 1-885266-41-3 (pbk.)
        I. Title.
    PS3560.A537Q4   1997
    811'.54—dc20   96-35008
                                                                         CIP

QUESTION FOR ECCLESIAST

POEMS BY
MARK JARMAN

STORY LINE PRESS
1997

ACKNOWLEDGEMENTS

AMERICAN POETRY REVIEW: Unholy Sonnets 5, 7, 11, 13, 17, 18 & 20

THE BLACK WARRIOR REVIEW: Unholy Sonnets 9 & 19

BOULEVARD: Proverbs

CRAZYHORSE: Upwelling; The Past from the Air

THE HUDSON REVIEW: Dressing My Daughters; Unholy Sonnets 1, 3, 6, 15 & 16

INDIANA REVIEW: Ground Swell

THE NEW CRITERION: Unholy Sonnets 2, 8, 10 & 14

NEW ENGLAND REVIEW: Wave; Questions for Ecclesiastes

THE NEW YORKER: A.M. Fog; In Front of the Children; Skin Cancer

PACIFIC REVIEW: After Disappointment; Stars

PLOUGHSHARES: Unholy Sonnet 4

POETRY NORTHWEST: To Zoë, Beginning Winter; Grid

SEWANEE THEOLOGICAL REVIEW: Transfiguration

SHENANDOAH: Last Suppers

THE SOUTHERN REVIEW: Unholy Sonnet 12

SOUTHWEST REVIEW: Drought Rain

THE THREEPENNY REVIEW: The Worry Bird

"Grid" appeared in *Pushcart XVII.* "Questions for Ecclesiastes" appeared in *Pushcart XVIII* and in *Best American Poetry 1993* (Scribners). "Ground Swell" appeared in *New American Poets of the Nineties* (David R. Godine, 1991). "Unholy Sonnets" 2, 8, 10 & 14 appeared in *Best American Poetry 1994* (Scribners).

My thanks to the John Simon Guggenheim Memorial Foundation and the National Endowment for the Arts for fellowships that were of assistance while I completed this book. And special thanks to Roy Gottfried who loaned me 5F60 in the Heard Library at Vanderbilt University where a number of these poems were written. "Unholy Sonnet 18" is for him. "Transfiguration" is for Michelle Boisseau. "Questions for Ecclesiastes" is for Judson Mitcham. "Last Suppers" is for Andrew Hudgins.

TABLE OF CONTENTS

For Claire and Zoë

And after the earthquake a fire;
but the LORD was not in the fire.
And after the fire a still small voice.

1 Kings 19:12

GROUND SWELL

Is nothing real but when I was fifteen,
Going on sixteen, like a corny song?
I see myself so clearly then, and painfully—
Knees bleeding through my usher's uniform
Behind the candy counter in the theater
After a morning's surfing; paddling frantically
To top the brisk outsiders coming to wreck me,
Trundle me clumsily along the beach floor's
Gravel and sand; my knees aching with salt.
Is that all that I have to write about?
You write about the life that's vividest.
And if that is your own, that is your subject.
And if the years before and after sixteen
Are colorless as salt and taste like sand—
Return to those remembered chilly mornings,
The light spreading like a great skin on the water,
And the blue water scalloped with wind-ridges,
And—what was it exactly?—that slow waiting
When, to invigorate yourself, you peed
Inside your bathing suit and felt the warmth
Crawl all around your hips and thighs,
And the first set rolled in and the water level
Rose in expectancy, and the sun struck
The water surface like a brassy palm,
Flat and gonglike, and the wave face formed.
Yes. But that was a summer so removed
In time, so specially peculiar to my life,
Why would I want to write about it again?

There was a day or two when, paddling out,
An older boy who had just graduated
And grown a great blonde moustache, like a walrus,
Skimmed past me like a smooth machine on the water,
And said my name. I was so much younger,
To be identified by one like him—
The easy deference of a kind of god
Who also went to church where I did—made me
Reconsider my worth. I had been noticed.
He soon was a small figure crossing waves,
The shawling crest surrounding him with spray,
Whiter than gull feathers. He had said my name
Without scorn, just with a bit of surprise
To notice me among those trying the big waves
Of the morning break. His name is carved now
On the black wall in Washington, the frozen wave
That grievers cross to find a name or names.
I knew him as I say I knew him, then,
Which wasn't very well. My father preached
His funeral. He came home in a bag
That may have mixed in pieces of his squad.
Yes, I can write about a lot of things
Besides the summer that I turned sixteen.
But that's my ground swell. I must start
Where things began to happen and I knew it.

I

TRANSFIGURATION

And there appeared to them Elijah and Moses
and they were talking to Jesus. Mark 9:2

1

They were talking to him about resurrection, about law,
    about the suffering ahead.
They were talking as if to remind him who he was and
    who they were. He was not
Like his three friends watching a little way off, not like
    the crowd
At the foot of the hill. A gray-green thunderhead massed
    from the sea
And God spoke from it and said he was his. They were
    talking
About how the body, broken or burned, could live again,
    remade.
Only the fiery text of the thunderhead could explain it.
    And they were talking
About pain and the need for judgement and how he would
    make himself
A law of pain, both its spirit and its letter in his own flesh,
    and then break it,
That is, transcend it. His clothes flared like magnesium,
    as they talked.

2

When we brought our mother to him, we said, "Lord,
    she falls down the stairs.
She cannot hold her water. In the afternoon she forgets
    the morning."
And he said, "All things are possible to those who believe.
    Shave her head,
Insert a silicone tube inside her skull, and run it under
    her scalp,
Down her neck, and over her collarbone, and lead it into
    her stomach."
And we did and saw that she no longer stumbled or wet
    herself.
She could remember the morning until the evening came.
    And we went our way,
Rejoicing as much as we could, for we had worried many
    years.

3

They were talking to him about heaven, how all forms
    there were luciform,
How the leather girdle and the matted hair, how the lice
    coursing the skin
And the skin skinned alive, blaze with perfection,
    the vibrance of light.
And they were talking about the complexities of blood
    and lymph,
Each component crowding the vessels, the body and
    the antibody,

And they were talking about the lamp burning in
    the skull's niche,
The eyes drinking light from within and light from
    without,
And how simple it is to see the future, if you looked at it
    like the past,
And how the present belonged to the flesh and its density
    and darkness
And was hard to talk about. Before and after were easier.
    They talked about light.

4

A man came to him who said he had been blind since
    his wedding day
And had never seen his wife under the veil or the children
    she had given him.
And the Lord said, "Tell me about your parents."
    And the man talked
A long time, remembering how his mother cut his father's
    meat at dinner,
And how at night their voices crept along his bedroom
    ceiling, like—
But he could not say what they were like. And in
    the morning, everything began to tick
And ticked all day as if.... Now, he remembered!
And suddenly his sight came back and blinded him, like
    a flashbulb.

5

They were talking to him about law and how lawgiving
    should be
Like rainfall, a light rain falling all morning and mixing
    with dew—
A rain that passes through the spiderweb and penetrates
    the dirt clod
Without melting it, a persistent, suffusing shower, soaking
    clothes,
Making sweatshirts heavier, wool stink, and finding every
    hair's root on the scalp.
And that is when you hurled judgement into the crowd
    and watched them
Spook like cattle, reached in and stirred the turmoil faster,
    scarier.
And they were saying that, to save the best, many must be
    punished,
Including the best. And no one was exempt, as they
    explained it,
Not themselves, not him, or anyone he loved, anyone who
    loved him.

6

Take anyone and plant a change inside them that they feel
And send them to an authority to assess that feeling.
        When they are told
That for them alone there waits a suffering in accordance
    with the laws

Of their condition, from which they may recover or may not,
Then they know the vortex on the mountaintop, the inside
    of the unspeakable,
The speechlessness before the voices begin talking to them,
Talking to prepare them, arm them and disarm them, until
    the end.
And if anybody's looking, they will seem transfigured.

7

I want to believe that he talked back to them, his radiant
    companions,
And I want to believe he said too much was being asked
    and too much promised.
I want to believe that that was why he shone in the eyes
    of his friends,
The witnesses looking on, because he spoke for them,
    because he loved them
And was embarrassed to learn how he and they were
    going to suffer.
I want to believe he resisted at that moment, when he
    appeared glorified,
Because he could not reconcile the contradictions
    and suspected
That love had a finite span and was merely the comfort
    of the lost.
I know he must have acceded to his duty, but I want
    to believe
He was transfigured by resistance, as he listened,
    and they talked.

P R O V E R B S

Three things are too wonderful for me;
Four I do not understand:
The way of an eagle in the sky,
The way of a serpent on a rock,
The way of a ship on the high seas,
And the way of a man with a maiden.
Proverbs 30:18–19

Three things are too wonderful for me;
Four I do not understand;
Five fill me with awe; six I love:
Our souls awake; our bodies awake;
The envelope of our tension;
The arcing cry of release;
The silence of the house at night;
The deep sleep of our children.

Three things are too wonderful for me—
Four I do not understand:
The child fading in the face bones;
Appetite and failure
Becoming distinct in the face;
Aging, its lightness and heaviness,
Floating away, sinking;
And the inner solitude,
The hermit brain, the heart like a recluse.

Most primitive, most original, first,
As blind with ego as a baby's fist,

The heart takes hold of speech,
     It takes and holds the word *heart*
And the thought, making both feel
     Their own pulse, their heart's life.

Three things wake me in the night—
     Four things at 3 a.m.:
Her absence from my side;
     The ceiling of time like an eyelid;
A child talking in sleep;
     The close knocking of a narrow space.

Three things erase the future—
     Four make the past a dream:
The entrance of God into history;
     The knowledge that now he is caught;
The temporary perfection
     Of lovers fitting together,
Going on and on for a moment;
     And the memory of that moment.

This is the way with daily life—
     From waking to sleeping is like this:
Morning rising lighter than air,
     And at midday, a shift, a tilting;
Then, the descent through clouds;
     The desire for another body;
And foundation again, weight
     Of the earth, the earth's core.

Three things are too wonderful for me—
     Four I do not understand:

The aching fabric of desire;
    The firmness, head to foot,
Of the absent one you need;
    The light her body is made of;
The gravity of light.

Three things name God—
    Four establish God's presence:
The inner voice saying *Live*;
    The outer voice saying *Live*;
The voice saying, "Oh, my God!"
    At the abrupt stoppage of time;
And repeating, like a psalm,
    "My whole body is moving."

DROUGHT RAIN

Rapturous, all day at the window,
Watching the return of life to earth,
Knowing these were last night's voices,
These were the cat-on-screen-door clawings,
These clear corpuscles, anatomies
Of visitants, Magi, holy children,
Entering the sand, slicking cracks
Like Vaseline, and closing them with mud,
Exalting and suspending in a dream
The whole day, making the world
Of dusty palm leaves, flammable eucalyptus,
Hiss, rattle, drink up with pleasure.
And no one to remember the last time
Such wonders occurred, when the salamander
Threaded inside a window frame to bask
On a lawn-lush strip of mildew,
And the toadstools, fed by seepage,
Appeared on the shag carpet.
Yet it was real and the rain came
On legs of its own walking off the ocean,
Wind-flanneled, tearing at hills,
Bringing down rooftop decorations and houses
That fell like faces, the caked earth smiling.
On flats below, the streets went under,
Strings of lights shorted out like firecrackers,
Ballfields bled through peepholes,
Cars died in fresh swamps of sky.
Afterwards, there were the sunken crèches,
The cardboard and paper barns along the boulevards,

Collapsed like shanties, and under overpasses,
The shanties, soaked and crumpled, still inhabited.
Guttings of storm surf on the public beaches,
Bait shops and picture windows emptied like buckets,
And those spectacular hillside cave-ins,
Making the rich homeless, too.
Sprayed trees sipped at their tap-water
Indoors. Dying needles, permanently green,
Grew sharper. Along the limbs,
Lights burned like a kind of dew, a wish
To see in the drying streets the advent
Of permanent renewal, a depth of change
In the new green mud, and not, a few days later,
The hurt haze of weed stems
In sidewalk cracks and vacant lots,
Like manger straw, pale as match flame.

DRESSING MY DAUGHTERS

One girl a full head taller
Than the other—into their Sunday dresses.
First, the slip, hardly a piece of fabric,
Softly stitched and printed with a bud.
I'm not their mother, and tangle, then untangle
The whole cloth—on backwards, have to grab it
Round their necks. But they know how to pull
Arms in, a reflex of being dressed,
And also, a child's faith. The mass of stuff
That makes the Sunday frocks collapses
In my hands and finds its shape, only because
They understand the drape of it—
These skinny keys to intricate locks.
The buttons are a problem
For a surgeon. How would she connect
These bony valves and stubborn eyelets?
The filmy dress revolves in my blind fingers.
The slots work one by one.
And when they're put together,
Not like puppets or those doll-saints
That bring tears to true believers,
But living children, somebody's real daughters,
They do become more real.
They say, "Stop it!" and "Give it back!"
And "I don't want to!" They'll kiss
A doll's hard features, whispering,
"I'm sorry." I know just why my mother
Used to worry. Your clothes don't keep
You close—it's nakedness.

Clad in my boots and holster,
I would roam with my six-gun buddies.
We dealt fake death to one another,
Fell and rolled in filth and rose,
Grimy with wounds, then headed home.
But Sunday... what was that tired explanation
Given for wearing clothes that
Scratched and shone and weighed like a slow hour?
That we should shine—in gratitude.
So, I give that explanation, undressing them,
And wait for the result.
After a day like Sunday, such a long one,
When they lie down, half-dead,
To be undone, they won't help me.
They cry, "It's not my fault."

TO ZOË, BEGINNING WINTER

There is one story and one story only.
        —Robert Graves

The ground, hard as a board this morning, thrusts up
Glassy nails in the garden,
The spikes of frozen humus, tipped with frost.
The gaudy proof of spring—that life is joy—
Bides its time dully, deeply.
In the warmth of the house, still you dress for summer.

You were born for glamour in this season, for darkened
        eyebrows,
Lipstick, outlandish hats,
To trail a filmy scarf through air and weave
The dance of a five-year-old around your parents,
To Klezmer music, jazz,
Beach Boys, Broadway show tunes, opera.

There is one story that won't be told here.
Skip this part until
You can imagine, in another winter,
Your cousins in the shifting ground of Poland,
Finding it hard to live.
Thinking of them, we always think of winter.

There is one story that won't be told here
And that is dying of cold.
Coming in from the cold your cheeks spice the air,
One eyebrow arches with your sense of drama,
Calling for tears or laughter—
We can't tell, until you laugh or cry.

A little bit of history is passing.
The age of your flamboyance
Burns brightly in your face and in our faces,
Now as the sun is born again and rises,
Not like a resurrection—
In glory all at once—but warily.

AFTER DISAPPOINTMENT

To lie in your child's bed when she is gone
Is calming as anything I know. To fall
Asleep, her books arranged above your head,
Is to admit that you have never been
So tired, so enchanted by the spell
Of your grown body. To feel small instead
Of blocking out the light, to feel alone,
Not knowing what you should or shouldn't feel,
Is to find out, no matter what you've said
About the cramped escapes and obstacles
You plan and face and have to call the world,
That there remain these places, occupied
By children, yours if lucky, like the girl
Who finds you here and lies down by your side.

WAVE

Always offshore, or already broken, gone;
Foaming around the skin;
Its print embedded in the rigid sand;
Rising from almost nothing on the beach
To show its brood of gravel,
Then coming down hard, making its point felt.

Saying, "This time I mean it. This time I will
Not have to do it over;"
Repeating as if to perfect, as if,
Repeated, each were perfect; all forgotten,
One by one by one;
Every one, monster or beauty, going smash.

Wall after falling wall out to the sunset;
Or the ugly freak, capsizing
The fishing boat, reforming, riding on;
Still beautiful, lifting the frond of kelp,
Holding the silversides
Up to the eye, coming ashore in dreams.

Coming to light; invisible, appearing
To be the skeleton
Of water, or its muscle, or the look
Crossing its face; intelligence or instinct
Or neither; all we see
In substance moving toward us, all we wish for.

Already rising, lump in the throat, pulse
That taps the fingertip;
The word made flesh, gooseflesh; placid, the skin,
Remembering the sudden agitation,
Swelling again with pleasure;
All riders lifted easily as light.

II

GRID

I walk those streets tonight, streets named for gems,
And streets that cross them named for Spanish women.
The gem streets end at the ocean, looking out.
Each woman wears a string of them and ends
With nothing on the edge of town. They are
Juanita, Inez, Maria, Lucia, Elena.
Their jewels are Opal, Emerald, Carnelian,
Topaz, Sapphire, Pearl, Ruby, Diamond.
I'm never sure I've named them all or walked
Along them all. Some are like boulevards.
Those are the gem streets. Some little more than lanes—
Those are the women. Yet I have searched for Opal
Among dead ends and alleys and discovered it
Dangling from Maria's wrist, or Juanita's.
All the life I care about, or almost all,
Lived first along these streets. That life is gone.
And when I say, "I walk those streets tonight,"
It's only poetry. I, too, am gone.
The streets maintain their urban grid, their limits.
The gem streets end at the ocean, the blank Pacific.
And the ones that wear them, named for Spanish women,
Themselves end on the edge of town with nothing.

QUESTIONS FOR ECCLESIASTES

What if on a foggy night in a beachtown, a night when
the Pacific leans close like the face of a wet cliff, a
preacher were called to the house of a suicide, a
house of strangers, where a child had discharged a
rifle through the roof of her mouth and the top of
her skull?

What if he went to the house where the parents, stunned
into plaster statues, sat behind their coffee table,
and what if he assured them that the sun would rise
and go down, the wind blow south, then turn north,
whirling constantly, rivers—even the concrete flume
of the great Los Angeles—run into the sea, and four-
teen year old girls would manage to spirit themselves
out of life, nothing was new under the sun?

What if he said the eye is not satisfied with seeing, nor the
ear filled with hearing? Would he want to view the
bedroom vandalized by self-murder or hear the
quiet before the tremendous shout of the gun or the
people inside the shout, shouting or screaming,
crying and pounding to get into the room, kicking
through the hollow-core door and making a new
sound and becoming a new silence—the silence he
entered with his comfort?

What if as comfort he said to the survivors I praise the
　　　dead which are dead already more than the living,
　　　and better is he than both dead and living who is
　　　not yet alive? What if he folded his hands together
　　　and ate his own flesh in prayer? For he did pray
　　　with them. He asked them, the mother and father, if
　　　they wished to pray to do so in any way they felt
　　　comfortable, and the father knelt at the coffee table
　　　and the mother turned to squeeze her eyes into a
　　　corner of the couch, and they prayed by first listen-
　　　ing to his prayer, then clawing at his measured
　　　cadences with tears (the man cried) and curses (the
　　　woman swore). What if, then, the preacher said be
　　　not rash with thy mouth and let not thine heart be
　　　hasty to utter anything before God:　for God is in
　　　heaven?

What if the parents collected themselves, then, and asked
　　　him to follow them to their daughter's room, and
　　　stood at the shattered door, the darkness of the
　　　room beyond, and the father reached in to put his
　　　hand on the light switch and asked if the comforter,
　　　the preacher they were meeting for the first time in
　　　their lives, would like to see the aftermath, and
　　　instead of recoiling and apologizing, he said that
　　　the dead know not anything for the memory of
　　　them is forgotten? And while standing in the hall-
　　　way, he noticed the shag carpet underfoot, like the
　　　fur of a cartoon animal, the sort that requires comb-
　　　ing with a plastic rake, leading into the bedroom,
　　　where it would have to be taken up, skinned off the

concrete slab of the floor, and still he said for their
love and hatred and envy are now perished, neither
have the dead any more portion for ever in anything
that is done under the sun?

What if as an act of mercy so acute it pierced the preacher's
skull and traveled the length of his spine, the man
did not make him regard the memory of his daugh-
ter as it must have filled her room, but guided the
wise man, the comforter, to the front door, with his
wife with her arms crossed before her in that ges-
ture we use to show a stranger to the door, acting
out a rite of closure, compelled to be social, as we
try to extricate ourselves by breaking off the exten-
sions of our bodies, as raccoons gnaw their legs from
traps, turning aside our gaze, letting only the numb
tissue of valedictory speech ease us apart, and the
preacher said live joyfully all the days of the life of
thy vanity, for that is thy portion in this life?

They all seem worse than heartless, don't they, these stark
and irrelevant platitudes, albeit stoical and final,
oracular, stony, and comfortless? But they were at
the center of that night, even if they were unspoken.

And what if one with only a casual connection to the
tragedy remembers a man, younger than I am today,
going out after dinner and returning, then sitting in
the living room, drinking a cup of tea, slowly
finding the strength to say he had visited these
grieving strangers and spent some time with them?

Still that night exists for people I do not know in ways I do not know, though I have tried to imagine them. I remember my father going out and my father coming back. The fog, like the underskin of a broken wave, made a low ceiling that the street lights pierced and illuminated. And God who shall bring every work into judgement, with every secret thing, whether it be good or whether it be evil, who could have shared what he knew with people who needed urgently to hear it, God kept a secret.

STARS

I signed up for astronomy in college
Just to be close to a girl
I lost before the course was over. She'd seen me
Walking below some cherry trees on campus.
"The world was blooming," she wrote.
"And you trudged through, looking at the ground."

The outrage this inspired in me was like
The solar wind I imagined—
Not the airy plasma of deep space,
But a righteous blast of heat. I telephoned
And roared it in her ear.
She answered, "You're not really mad at me."

To this day I get taken by surprise.
I look up and the world
Is clotted with snow or flowers, stars have pricked
The breathless, late, blue evening sky, my children
Have tiptoed in beside me,
And my response is "Please! Leave me alone!"

Then, I have to say, "Don't listen to me."
I repeat it to myself,
"Don't listen." And I still confuse the rain,
Seething across a parking lot at dusk,
And the other inner downpour
That I shake off with a curse and an excuse.

I want to be like you, poised, placid stars,
Too far away to threaten
With your own throbbing storms and fields of force,
Like you, like lights pinned to a sphere of glass
Turned by love itself—
To give up to your peace, turned by love.

UPWELLING

Under the wave, the gray, clamping pressure—

Strange, in that moment, to remember, posed
Beside a pavement sapling with a girl
Who feared and loved him, Kevin Horrigan,
His face like a manhole cover, his crime coming
With a tire iron clanging on a can lid,
Still wanting, in that moment, something nice.

Under tons of foam, palms pressed, chest down on sand—

And still to wonder how a kiss would taste,
If only she would come down here and press
Her body close, but with a softer pressure.
Passing a word between her lips, into
A cloud of longing, she kisses air goodbye.
Felicia Smith—she kisses air goodbye.

Eyes stung, breath held in the down-rush, then—

To know the heart of Johnny Lopez, suddenly,
Changed overnight from boy to brooding man,
No way to bring him back, coiling laughter
Around and round his fist like a wet rag,
The laughter of boys—to know his coiled heart,
To feel it, and the sudden end of childhood,

Like bringing down the house to shut a suitcase.

And now the morning wells up from a dream,
A face lies close, and there are children waking,
Like echoes, in another room. The past
Folds back into the past, and out of sleep,
The streaming peace below the wave, you come
(You... you. Who *are* you?)—

Suspended, like a sentence, in the present.

A.M. F O G

Night's afterbirth, last dream before waking,
Holding on with dissolving hands,
Out of it came, not a line of old men,
But pairs of headlights, delaying morning.

It felt like tears, like wetted bedsheets,
And suspended in it like a medicine
In vapor was the ocean's presence, ghost
Of deep water and the bite of salt.

Here you found your body again,
The hand before your face and the face it touched,
Eyes floating, feet on invisible ground,
Vagueness like another skin.

Sent out into it anyway, because it was morning,
To taste it, touch blind hardness
Like marble ruins, and skirt the edges,
Razors in goosedown, hydrants' fists.

Abruptly out of it waves appeared,
Transmuted from hanging silver ore, crafted
Before the eyes into curving metals
That broke into soup scum, Queen Anne's lace.

Out of a great nothing, a theology.
Out of the amorphous, an edgeless body
Or one like a hunting mass of tendrils
That hurried down the sand, moved by hunger.

I remember a gang of friends
Racing a fog bank's onslaught along the beach.
Seal-slick, warm from the sun
This thing would eat, they ran laughing.

The fog came on. And they were beautiful,
The three boys and one girl, still in her wetsuit,
And the dissolution overtaking them,
Their stridency, full of faith, still audible.

All morning bathed in a dovelike brooding.
The fog satisfied itself by overwhelming
The meagre dew, watering the doors
Of snails, the leeward mold, and held still.

And then near noon there was a concentration
As if the sky tried to find a slippery word
Or remember—*that's right*—remember
Where it was in an unfamiliar bedroom.

And knew. And switched the light on. Wide awake.

III

UNHOLY SONNETS

1

Dear God, Our Heavenly Father, Gracious Lord,
Mother Love and Maker, Light Divine,
Atomic Fingertip, Cosmic Design,
First Letter of the Alphabet, Last Word,
Mutual Satisfaction, Cash Award,
Auditor Who Approves Our Bottom Line,
Examiner Who Says That We Are Fine,
Oasis That All Sands Are Running Toward.

I can say almost anything about you,
O Big Idea, and with each epithet,
Create new reasons to believe or doubt you,
Black Hole, White Hole, Presidential Jet.
But what's the anything I must leave out? You
Solve nothing but the problems that I set.

2

Hands folded to construct a church and steeple,
A roof of knuckles, outer walls of skin,
The thumbs as doors, the fingers bent within
To be revealed, wriggling, as "all the people,"
All eight of them, enmeshed, caught by surprise,
Turned upward blushing in the sudden light,
The nails like welders' masks, the fit so tight
Among them you can hear their half-choked cries
To be released, to be pried from this mess
They're soldered into somehow—they don't know.
But stuck now they are willing to confess,
If that will ease your grip and let them go,
Confess the terror they cannot withstand
Is being locked inside another hand.

3

Balaam upon his ass was unaware
That he was not completely in control
Or that his own ego was not his soul.
His ass, however, knew enough to fear
The figure standing in the thoroughfare.
God opened the ass's mouth so she could tell
Balaam, who could not see the obstacle,
That striking her, as he had, was unfair.

I want like Balaam to be shown my soul.
His was a donkey blessed with second sight,
Endowed with speech to limn the invisible.
And mine—will it rear up in holy fright
Or stall before the garage doors of hell?
I need a metaphor to sleep tonight.

4

Amazing to believe that nothingness
Surrounds us with delight and lets us be,
And that the meekness of nonentity,
Despite the friction of the world of sense,
Despite the leveling of violence,
Is all that matters. All the energy
We force into the matchhead and the city
Explodes inside a loving emptiness.

Not Dante's rings, not the Zen zero's mouth,
Out of which comes and into which light goes,
This God recedes from every metaphor,
Turns the hardest data into untruth,
And fills all blanks with blankness. This love shows
Itself in absence, which the stars adore.

5

This is the moment. This is all we have.
But how can we say this? What do we mean
By saying this to children, like sad men
With minds gone rotten in a sexual hive,
Who show children the secret thing they have—
The answer to all questions? What do we mean,
Then, by the souls of children, women, men?
The question stung and swollen in the hive.
I think I know sometimes and feel the joy
Of loving only for a lifetime. Death
Will smoke us out like bees, but we'll forget
That we were going to see the end of joy.
Our souls will keep like honey after death.
We'll forget that we were going to forget.

6

Look into the darkness and the darkness looks—
As if it massed before a telescope
Or turned because behind it heard your step—
The darkness looks at you. This idea spooks
Some people, and their reason self-destructs.
Seized by a love of daylight, back they jump
Into the known, blazing like a headlamp,
Into the senses tuned like cars and trucks.

And what about the counsel of my friend
Who says that when we look for God, remember
God looks for us? If that's what starts the thing,
Then we must drive in circles till we find
It's all one. To be looked for is to look for.
And seeing is believing and being seen.

7

Reduce the proof of nature. So we tried
And still found that our bodies kept their faith.
Reduce the body, burn away the brain.
We tried and found the chemical debris
Inscribed with calculations of a mind.
Reduce the compounds, elements, all bits
Of matter, energy. Make all abstract.
We tried and met the idea of the act.
But what was that? Without prerequisites
Of... you know what I mean. We couldn't find...
What's the word for it? We couldn't see...
But any metaphor will seem inane.
Without the world, we met the death
Of God. And language. Both of them had died.

8

Two forces rule the universe of breath
And one is gravity and one is light.
And does their jurisdiction include death?
Does nothingness exist in its own right?
It's hard to say, lying awake at night,
Full of an inner weight, a glaring dread,
And feeling that Simone Weil must be right.
Two forces rule the universe, she said,
And they are light and gravity. And dead,
She knows, as you and I do not, if death
Is also ruled or if it rules instead,
And if it matters, after your last breath.
But she said truth was on the side of death
And thought God's grace filled emptiness, like breath.

9

Almighty God, to you all hearts are open,
All throats, all voice boxes, all inner ears,
All pupils, all tear ducts, all cavities
Inside the skull inside the trick of flesh.
To you the face is like a picture window,
The body is a door of molded glass,
All lengths of gut are pasture, all membrane
Peels back and off like ripe persimmon skin.
And every wrinkle folded in the brain
Runs smoothly through your fingers and snaps back
Into its convolution. Even the blood
Is naked as a bolt of oilcloth.
You touch the working parts and track the thought,
A comet on your fingertip, and squint.

10

Time to admit my altar is a desk.
Time to confess the cross I bear a pen.
My soul, a little like a compact disc,
Slides into place, a laser plays upon
Its surface, and a sentimental mist,
Freaked with the colors of church window glass,
Rides down a shaft of light that smells of must
As music adds a layer of high gloss.
Time to say plainly when I am alone
And waiting for the coming of the ghost
Whose flame-tongue like a blow torch, sharp and lean,
Writes things that no one ever could have guessed,
I give in to my habit and my vice
And speak as soon as I can find a voice.

11

Half asleep in prayer I said the right thing
And felt a sudden pleasure come into
The room or my own body. In the dark,
Charged with a change of atmosphere, at first
I couldn't tell my body from the room.
And I was wide awake, full of this feeling,
Alert as though I'd heard a doorknob twist,
A drawer pulled, and instead of terror knew
The intrusion of an overwhelming joy.
I had said thanks and this was the response.
But how I said it or what I said it for
I still cannot recall and I have tried
All sorts of ways all hours of the night.
Once was enough to be dissatisfied.

12

There was a pious man upright as Job,
In fact, more pious, more upright, who prayed
The way most people thoughtlessly enjoy
Their stream of consciousness. He concentrated
On glorifying God, as some men let
Their minds create and fondle curving shadows.
And as he gained in bumper crops and cattle,
He greeted each success with grave amens.

So he was shocked, returning from the bank,
To see a flood bearing his farm away—
His cows, his kids, his wife, and all his stuff.
Swept off his feet, he cried out, "Why?" and sank.
And God grumped from his rain cloud, "I can't say.
Just something about you pisses me off."

13

Drunk on the Umbrian hills at dusk and drunk
On one pink cloud that stood beside the moon,
Drunk on the moon, a marble smile, and drunk,
Two young Americans, on one another,
Far from home and wanting this forever—
Who needed God? We had our bodies, bread,
And glasses of a raw, green, local wine,
And watched our Godless perfect darkness breed
Enormous softly burning ancient stars.
Who needed God? And why do I ask now?
Because I'm older and I think God stirs
In details that keep bringing back that time,
Details that are just as vivid now—
Our bodies, bread, a sharp Umbrian wine.

14

After the praying, after the hymn-singing,
After the sermon's trenchant commentary
On the world's ills, which make ours secondary,
After communion, after the hand-wringing,
And after peace descends upon us, bringing
Our eyes up to regard the sanctuary
And how the light swords through it, and how, scary
In their sheer numbers, motes of dust ride, clinging—
There is, as doctors say about some pain,
Discomfort knowing that despite your prayers,
Your listening and rejoicing, your small part
In this communal stab at coming clean,
There is one stubborn remnant of your cares
Intact. There is still murder in your heart.

15

A useful God will roost in a bird-box,
Wedge-head thrust out, red-feathered in the sun,
Each huge eye squinting through a minus sign,
His stiffened wakefulness, like a bird book's
Audubon print, hiding his claws' and beak's
Readiness to enjoy their work and soon.
A God like that will watch us think of sin,
Tilting his head, before he shrugs and backs
Away inside, leaving an empty hole.
Something of nature for the neighborhood,
Charming in daylight, while the pose is held...
We know, of course, in darkness rats are harried,
Moles are dismembered, and their screams are horrid.
A God like that can make the nighttime hell.

16

We drove to the world's end and there betrayed
The ones we promised not to. While we drove
We talked about the afterlife and love,
Slowing to an impatient crawl, delayed
By roadwork, in an idling parade
We couldn't see the head or tail of.
We inched past miles of asphalt, reeking stuff,
Stroked by a rake of fire as it was laid.
And we agreed the analogues for hell
Came to us everywhere we looked in life.
But not for heaven. For it we couldn't find
A metaphor or likeness. Not until
We had betrayed our loved ones, at the end,
Did we have something to compare it with.

17

God like a kiss, God like a welcoming,
God like a hand guiding another hand
And raising it or making it descend,
God like the pulse point and its silent drumming,
And the tongue going to it, God like the humming
Of pleasure if the skin felt it as sound,
God like the hidden wanting to be found
And like the joy of being and becoming.
And God the understood, the understanding,
And God the pressure trying to relieve
What is not pain but names itself with weeping,
And God the rush of time and God time standing,
And God the touch body and soul believe,
And God the secret neither one is keeping.

18

In *Civilization and Its Discontents*
Freud quotes the poet Heine in a footnote
That's *Schadenfreude* incarnate. Heine wrote
(Although I'm playing loosely with the sense):
"My needs are few and my desires but these—
A woodland house, the best of simple food,
And just outside my door, if God is good,
Some six or seven of my enemies,
Strung up so as to make my heart swell full.
Before they died, I would forgive them all
The wrongs they'd done me—grant them absolution.
For to do on earth as it is done in heaven,
I know one's enemies must be forgiven,
But not before they're brought to execution."

19

I swat him in the face and hope that nothing
Comes of it. Then much later, late at night,
Lying in my oblong of insomnia,
Ask for forgiveness in the form of sleep.
I hope that nothing will arouse him further,
That nothing will hurt him further, but I know,
At the top of the fenced walkway, he is waiting,
An offended fifteen-year-old with a man's fists
That come at me like bulletins, like headlines.
I will not sleep tonight. I will not sleep.
God can be hurt, the vast is vulnerable,
The infinite capacity to love can weep,
Then turn away, the dark side of the sun,
Discovered at the moment you are lost.

20

If God survives us, will his kingdom come?
But let's row out to sea and ship the oars
And watch the planet drown in meteors.
If God forgives us, surely he will come.
Can we nail up a man and do the same
To a child? Yes. And drive the spikes through tears.
But let's row out to sea and watch the stars.
No matter what we do, they are the same,
Crossing the bleeding sky on shining feet,
Walking on water toward us, and then sinking.
Surely when he grew up, God must have known
What sort of death was waiting for one thinking
That with his coming history was complete.
We'll greet him as the children would have done.

I V

IN FRONT OF THE CHILDREN

The children will be terrified, we know it.
We remember how it was to see
The bald eyes set in muscle, and the masks
Put back on quickly, never fitting right,
Over the sinew of our parents' faces.

That look, that word, that slow or sudden gesture—
One day the boys and girls will know what happened.
One day they will begin articulately
To gossip among themselves, with God, with strangers,
With the names changed to pronouns for protection.

She said it right outloud so we could hear it.
He did that and then he looked at us.

Hearing the phrase in a cafeteria spoken
By one parent to another—"in front of the children"—
I remember how it came to mean what it means,
Because we heard it said and now we say it,
Though everything has been done.

SKIN CANCER

Balmy overcast nights of late September;
Palms standing out in street light, house light;
Full moon penetrating the cloud-film
With an explosive halo, a ring almost half the sky;
Air like a towel draped over shoulders;
Lightness or gravity deferred like a moral question;
The incense in the house lit; the young people
Moving from the front door into the half-dark
And back, or up the stairs to glimpse the lovers' shoes
Outside the master bedroom; the youngest speculating;
The taste of beer, familiar as salt water;
Each window holding a sea view, charcoal
With shifting bars of white; the fog filling in
Like the haze of distance itself, pushing close, blurring.

As if the passage into life were through such houses,
Surrounded by some version of ocean weather,
Lit beads of fog or wind so stripped it burns the throat;
Mildew-spreading, spray-laden breezes and the beach sun
Making each grain of stucco cast a shadow;
An ideal landscape sheared of its nostalgia;
S. with his black hair, buck teeth, unsunned skin,
Joking and disappearing; F. doing exactly the same
But dying, a corkscrew motion through green water;
And C. not looking back from the car door,
Reappearing beside the East River, rich, owned, smiling
        at last.

Swains and nymphs. And news that came with the sea damp,
Of steady pipe-corrosions, black corners,
Moisture working through sand lots, through slab floors,
Slowly, with chemical, with molecular intricacy,
Then, bursting alive: the shrieked confessions
Of the wild parents; the cliff collapse; the kidnap;
The cache of photos; the letter; the weapon; the haunted
        dream;
The sudden close-up of the loved one's degradation.

Weather a part of it all, permeating and sanctifying,
Infiltrating and destroying; the sun disc,
Cool behind the veil of afternoon cloud,
With sun spots like flies crawling across it;
The slow empurpling of skin all summer;
The glorious learned flesh and the rich pallor
Of the untouched places in the first nakedness;
The working of the lesion now in late life,
Soon to be known by the body, even the one
Enduring the bareness of the inland plains,
The cold fronts out of Canada, a sickness
For home that feels no different from health.

THE PAST FROM THE AIR

1. THE FALL

She holds her baby and steps into the air,
Looking beyond at waves, feeling the sun
Greet her outside the trailer. She is young
And pretty and unbalanced on the stair.
Her loving husband, fanning the firepit,
Her little boy, no more than three years old,
Stand barefoot in the sand and watch her fold
The baby in her arms and try to sit,
Then thrust the burden out like a full tray
She knows is going to topple, as the flight
Of flimsy steps tips sideways. She can't quite
Save the baby and herself, so she gives way
And curls into a miracle of falling,
The inverse of a cat, landing to buffer
The baby with herself. For years she'll suffer
The ugly proudflesh of the leg-gash, galling
In seaside dampness, fogs, and drizzling mists,
And keeping its strange pallor in the summer.
They drive a hundred miles for drugs to numb her.
The baby holds her torn blouse in its fists.
But the falling isn't over. It's beginning—
Past the recovery, that will take so long
Because her family needs her to be strong,
And past her husband's first, tentative sinning,
The stitching up of those first marriage rents,
Past years when he is honest with his wife,

Then past the children as they make her life
Their past and make their own lives present tense.
And when the falling does come to a stop,
May the earth that felt so firm beneath her feet,
Past love, and death of love, and self-deceit,
Falling itself through space still hold her up.

2. THE IRON

The day blew in the window from the sea
Through the wire mesh, its harp, and filled the room
With no sound louder than the soft TV
Or light too great to quell the little gloom,
The necessary shade to see the screen.
She stood beside the ironing board and hushed
The wind and pushed the iron, then paused to glean
Some word her own work noises might have crushed.

I lay on the leather couch, drowsy with flu,
And didn't wonder why the sea breeze entered,
Breaking my fever. All that I could do
Was pull my blanket up and watch the centered
Woman detest her work, untangle shirts
Lewdly embracing trouser legs and spit
At the hot iron and wind clump-end skirts
Of ravelled thread that she brought close and bit.

Somebody sang a song that made her frown
After the song was over and declare
That she believed it. She put the iron down,
Letting it rear up on its heel and glare,
And arched her back and gave her hips a twist
And looked out where the green peninsula
Bulked like a loaf of bread. Against the cliffs,
Gulls bent their wings like gulls a child would draw.

The TV kept on talking, but the song
Lingered because my mother made it stay
(She had the power to make life short or long),

Made it a thing to think about, to play
Back for its simple melody and words.
It said that no one could take what was hers,
What she loved, and said it to driving chords.
Wind, gulls, my fever—we were all believers.

3. THE MOMENT

Before the night-backed mirror of the window
Two faces act a moment; one a mother's,
Turned in enraptured focus; and the other,
Her son's, right angled to her, not wanting to know
That she is making up his face again
Out of the oil and water of the eye.
The torture of a gaze so lovingly
Projected at him petrifies her son.

She looks at him; he won't look back to her
In any way that shows acknowledgment,
Except in sidelong, stiff embarrassment,
Waiting for her to break off her sweet stare,
Her unself-conscious worship of the thing
He is, less linked than at his birth, less hers,
And safely distant, like remembered tears.
It's separateness itself she praises—being.

And he's too young to know it and, because young,
He wishes to be cruel for revenge,
As if she'd called his name among his friends
And called him home or, worse, had called him handsome.
He tries to call her bluff; he tries to squeeze
All his attention to the dish he's drying.
(They're doing dishes.) Perhaps, she will start crying
If he does look at her. He feels her eyes.

What does it mean to feel a person's eyes?
It is a sudden stillness, the halt of one
That was in motion with another, then

The watched one feeling his own muscles freeze,
As if his skin had eyelids and they opened
Under a gaze that blinded. Now he turns
Bravely to meet her love; he smiles and turns.
And she smiles, but her revery has ended.

4. PRAYING

A wedge of morning sunshine bathes her hands.
The suds mount breeding like a hive of foam.
A bowl laden with floating steam descends
Into the underwater catacomb
Of crockery and silver, where the wands
Of fingers do their work. The plates become
Immaculate as halos. Then, the rack
Receives them; dried, they're piled into a stack.

She's praying as she does this, as she soaks
A sponge with liquid soap and looks outside,
Handling the chore, scrubbing the hardened yolks
And coffee stains, as if preoccupied
With one cloud breaking sunlight into spokes.
She's praying though her eyes are open wide.
She's doing three things, watching a cloud pass,
Talking to God, drying a drinking glass.

It is a perfect time to be alone
And easier, alone, to pray for those
Who've left her with the silent chaperone
Of the sun, watching through the kitchen windows,
Making the noise of work an undertone.
The image of her loved ones forms and grows
Like foam riddled with light. She holds it still,
A solid thing, for God to gaze his fill.

And what God sees, if God sees anything,
Looks like the crawling colors on a bubble
Before it breaks and drops a filmy rain

On someone's palm. He sees the vivid scrawl
Of light across creation, but no sign
Of prayer, which is abstract, invisible.
He sees a woman asking him to read
Her mind. He pities her. He cannot read.

5. PATIENCE

One of those days the traveller doesn't call.
One of those mornings, afternoons, and nights
The farflung husband has forgotten all
The distance he has left her with. She works
Inside the house and out. Her children watch
And learn the ritual for killing time:
Make simple tasks more intricate. They catch
The drift that carries them through long weekends.

It could be worse; the world could rub it in,
Withholding light and warmth, keeping back color.
But sadness for the Californian,
Living beside broad beaches of white sand,
Must be endured in sunshine, under palms,
Among yucca flowers, exploding fuchsias,
And with an ocean given to vast calms,
Swelling inside with something that won't break.

She can replant the rotting ivy bed,
Searching along each runner to its root,
As if back through a sequence in her head,
And spend an hour on the origin
Of one impacted strand. She can unearth
Wads of redemption stamps, Blue Chip and Green,
From bottom drawers, and sit beside the hearth
Of the TV, licking one stamp at a time.

The call will come. She knows his call will come.
Meanwhile, she works and answers children's questions.
Today, one question is, "Why is God dumb?"

She pauses. Dumb? And puts a stamp in place.
"Yes," says the child. "All I can hear is silence
After I pray." Inside she notes the challenge:
If God does not exist, describe his absence.
No word. No word. No word. No word. No word.

6. THE APPARITION

The old trees of the neighborhood are dying.
Entire limbs have torn off hackberries.
The redbuds have gone hollow. And the blades
Of tree surgeons are busy. It has been
Two years since we last walked here, looking for
Nothing so much as things to talk about.
The sun and rain have made streets dark and light
In jigsaw patterns. Winter's almost here.

In fact, it is here, has been for two days.
Gulf air, we guess, has pushed Canadian
Out from beneath the mellow Christmas sun.
The barbed cold front has tangled in the trees
Of Tennessee, and rain has turned them green
Where molds and lichens, mosses, sheathe their bark.
White fungus florets dot a twig, rain-black
And broken at my feet, two fingers long.

I pick it up and quote some poetry,
Because it looks like Pound's similitude
For the incandescent faces in the crowd,
"Petals on a wet, black bough," in the subway.
My mother holds the glistening stick of locust
And responds, sighing, that indeed she sees,
But not the pale spring blossoms in Pound's eyes.
She sees the faces only and the darkness.

She sees my face (It's time to change the subject!)
As I came running home across the lawn
One night. The voice and body of her son,

Which as she heard me calling had been separate,
Joined in the porchlight, asking for forgiveness.
What had I done? Only stayed out past dinner.
But what a dark deed then, that distant summer.
How white our faces both were with distress.

7. THE PAST FROM THE AIR

The view the book gives is anonymous.
The pastel condominiums, the water,
Wearing a sheen that looks ingenuous
(The way a stranger might ask, "Is this your daughter?"),
Offer a kind of clue that you might miss
Unless determined to locate the place.
Clairvoyance takes on the power of the wish
And recognition is an act of grace.

But there it is, as if unsheeted, bare,
Waiting to be identified, it spoke
Softly and drew you closer by the hair
And said its own name, laughing at the joke.
My mother sitting next to me looks on,
Arms folded as if to heal two bitten hands.
I point the landmarks out, the known, unknown,
Unpeopled, sun-slick, like the glossy sands.

She has no reason to remember this
Declining beachtown where she was not young
With any sort of love or happiness
Or now, to see it renovated, sprung
To a new level of well-being, grow
Nostalgic as her son does. Home
Is nothing to be sick for, when you know
It is an idea sculpted out of foam.

And now I see she only looks askance,
Folded away as if the open book
Could trap her or the place had burned her once,

And that it would be cruel to make her look
Beyond the page, that only shows the beach
And dwellings bright above it and the pier.
What the imagination brought in reach
Would be more than a house. We leave it there.

LAST SUPPERS

Loneliest when hung in a church annex,
Like a No Smoking sign, itself ablaze.
In the faithful reproductions the deterioration
Hangs like religious haze in the Upper Room.

Times I have noticed it was present fix
And obliterate the rooms where it was hung.
The scene so intimate in its dismay,
Familiar as a family's daily warfare.

What has happened? It's as if dinner has ended
With Father drunk again and Mother silent.
The daughters are enlisted to clean up.
They leave. And the sons begin to fight.

But, no. Christ has forecast his betrayal.
The group gesticulates, the traitor shrinks,
Spilling the salt for bad luck. And the meal
Is not finished, still has to be eaten.

*

I knew a family who hung a Last Supper
Above their dining table. A box of glass,
Like an aquarium of fish and weed,
With a lightbulb to turn the colors on.

I don't have to picture them together.
I've sat in their bitter circle, underneath
The lit-up masterpiece, heartsick, knowing
Dessert was the old man's fist against his eldest

And down the punching order to my friend.
Septic with unshed tears, he would turn on me,
And yet not bring himself to raise his fist.
His younger sister would stand up on a chair,

As Jesus and his apostles were switched off,
And point and say, "That's God." You had to answer
Before the scene went dark. You had to say,
"Yes," to her catechism. "That is God."

*

A child, I was brought into a room,
Geometrical with shadows, in Milan,
And a chill like an embrace from underground.
Our silence was a reverence for a picture.

There was the great painting behind a rope
And a parental awe I couldn't share.
I was impressed by the museum photograph
Of the bombed church and the story of survival.

The copy that we bought was done on silk.
As precious as a prayer shawl, it would hang
Beside my father's desk at church, its colors
Ancient in the fluorescent, humming light.

Alone once, going through his desk, I found
Capsules of ammonia in silk sacks,
Aids for someone who dealt with the poor in spirit,
Cracked one, and felt my head snap back.

*

The irony and genius of the thing
Is that it does not look at us. The foreground
Figures are obsessed with one another.
A landscape watches them through distant windows.

Everywhere it appears, in books, in rooms,
The painting turns it subjects toward their Lord
And one another. Their gestures sing a hymn
Of self-importance. And he averts his eyes.

On our side, the world runs through its days
Or, if you wish, it braids in endless spirals.
And what we occupy or set in motion
Jars or meshes. When we pause to look outside,

Pictures look back at us and words respond,
Images return our human gaze.
But this, despite the copying, resists.
What matters is the loneliness of God.

*

Everyone knows the silence like a wind
You have to crouch in to eat your food in safety,
Or the outburst that rains poison on the supper,
Or dining alone, in your room or with a book.

Mother coming to the table piping hot
And Father on the rocks cranky with bourbon.
The children sensing the collision coming,
Sullen themselves, urging it to happen.

The reaction could as easily take place
While getting in the car or getting out,
Around the Christmas tree or television.
All it needs is a family's critical mass.

And yet the table is a raft to cling to.
Becalmed, each pins down an unsteady edge.
And when the swell, anger, rolls through the meal,
The inner cry is "Save yourself, if you can!"

*

I have a memory of Passover,
Crackling with an air of irritation.
We feared Elijah would enrage the host,
If he appeared at all, by being late.

To put our figures back into that evening,
The young couples, the parents, the empty chair,
Risks the restorer's bungling that can hasten
Collapse. Better to say, "We ate together."

And not that one kept looking at his plate.
One drank several glasses of sweet wine.
There was a moment nobody would speak.
Two fell out of love across the table.

Now the scene only retains its lines.
Color and character—the eyes, for example—
Are lost in clouds of crumbled memory.
Whole areas—the room, the year—have vanished.

*

The tumult of the twelve thrusts out a snaking
Embrace to clutch us close and feel the pressure
Of our belief or nonbelief. It pulls,
In either case, the eye close to the faces.

And most of them are marred beyond belief.
They fade in the pointillism of decay,
Like blown-up newspaper photography.
What moves us in the remnants? Common pathos.

Leonardo set the catastrophe in motion
By giving himself time to work slowly,
Thus mixed a base that let him perfect details.
In making the picture right he made it mortal.

Most copies restore exact lines and colors,
Unsubtly, like parade floats or modern
Translations of translations of the Bible.
But the crudest replica can smell of blood.

*

In the original the decay is like a smoke cloud,
Materializing from the walls and ceiling.
Someone, by now, should have called out, "Fire!"
And someone has, the calm one, at the center.

He has said it sadly, "Fire," and those hearing
Confer among themselves and make petitions
To ascertain if the announcement's really true.
Looked at thus they look ridiculous.

But as the smoke clears, they're not what I see,
Seized in their poses by a passion's heat.
I see a family's uninspired tableau,
Touched for once by a deep tranquillity.

They link hands, close eyes, pass a loving pressure,
Safe from disasters only God and Art
Would call down on their heads. When their eyes open,
They eat and drink and talk, at ease, in peace.

V

THE WORRY BIRD

God was an idea before he was an image.
And yet there are things like the worry bird
That stay with us through life and intercede
With an old darkness, filling an old need.
Hunched on a plaster base, a buffoon buzzard,
Like a firesale souvenir or piece of flood damage,
With a ruff of blue duck-down, and a rubber beak
Like a gray sock between its hang-dog eyes,
It stood beseechingly at the bedside.
"Don't be silly," they told us when we cried,
"Give your worries to the worry bird." Its gaze,
A weary martyr's, listened to us speak
As we learned patiently to say our prayers
That also left us lying in the dark,
Fringed with the light seeping under a door.
Though childhood fills with gaps as we get older,
The worry bird remains, with its wry look
And slumped wing shoulders, sagging with old cares:
The half hour they were late home from their party,
The lies told at school, accumulating,
The broken heirloom hidden in a drawer,
All things we don't think much of anymore,
Replaced by the grown world's escalating
Nightmares about career, money, duty.
The worry bird was meant to make us smile
As they smiled at our miniature infernos.
We know now they were right. And in their beds,
As we now know since we've seen inside their heads,
They had no silly icon for their troubles—

Only an idea, if at all. Meanwhile,
The worry bird takes on another form
And watches with another shade of interest,
Circling among the other distant images
That used to help and still do. Mirages
Of comfort, they can bring a kind of rest
Anyone who has been a child can know.